Signatures

Newfoundland Women Artists and Writers

Signatures

Newfoundland Women Artists and Writers

Killick Press
St. John's, Newfoundland
1996

Appreciation is expressed to *The Canada Council* for publication assistance.

The publisher acknowledges the financial contribution of the *Department of Tourism and Culture, Government of Newfoundland and Labrador,* which has helped make this publication possible.

Eastern Edge is a non-profit, artist-run gallery supported by the Canada Council, the Newfoundland and Labrador Arts Council, the City of St. John's, the Canada/Newfoundland Cooperation Agreement on Cultural Industries, the Department of Employment and Labour Relations, Human Resources Development Canada, private donations and the donated energy of volunteers.

∝ Printed on acid-free paper

Cover Design: Tara Bryan

Cover Photo: Dr. George A. Jenner
The cover image is a photo micrograph of a rare volcanic rock called boninite, named after the Bonin Islands off Japan. This rock is a signature of special plate tectonic conditions, and older equivalents of these rocks are preserved in a number of localities in central and western Newfoundland, signifying the same special conditions here 400 to 500 million years ago.

Published by
KILLICK PRESS
an imprint of Creative Book Publishing
A Division of 10366 Newfoundland Limited
A Robinson-Blackmore Printing & Publishing associated company
P.O. Box 8660, St. John's, Newfoundland A1B 3T7

Printed in Canada by:
ROBINSON-BLACKMORE PRINTING & PUBLISHING

Canadian Cataloguing in Publication Data

Main entry under title:

Signatures

Edited by Carmelita McGrath

ISBN 1-895387-66-3

1. Art, Modern — 20th century — Newfoundland — Exhibitions.
2. Art, Canadian — Newfoundland — Exhibitions.
3. Women Artists — Newfoundland — Exhibitions.
4. Canadian Literature (English) — Newfoundland — women authors.*
5. Canadian literature (English) — Newfoundland — 20th century.*
I. McGrath, Carmelita

N6546.N45S54 1996   700'.9718'0747181   C96-950028-9

A project of Eastern Edge Gallery

Writing

Works of Art

Introduction

Signatures, Eastern Edge Gallery, February 25 -March 26, 1996

Since its inception in 1984, Eastern Edge Gallery has held an annual Women's Day exhibition with the intent to pay tribute to women creators. One year ago, it was decided that for 1996 Eastern Edge would invite ten prominent Newfoundland women writers to produce new literary works in response to the visual art of a Newfoundland woman artist of their choice. The result— *Signatures: Newfoundland Women Artists and Writers,* an exhibition at Eastern Edge and this publication.

Art and literature, image and text, have long shared a history. Art has played a complementary role to literature through illustration. However, art does not merely serve a subordinate function to literature. In *Signatures,* the work of visual artists, chosen by the writers, is the impetus or inspiration for the creation of poetry, prose and fiction. Art and literature present two sides of a dialogue, partners in communication and expression. Indeed, many of the writers own the works they have chosen to include in the exhibition.

By inviting another discipline to collaborate in an exhibition, Eastern Edge is fostering communication and openness among the arts, offering new and exciting opportunities to creators and the public alike. Eastern Edge is pleased to be able to present this publication as a record of *Signatures,* which will no doubt become an important document of women artists and writers in Newfoundland in our time.

In the spirit of Women's Day, these women chose to work together, focusing on the similarity, strength or commonality they found in their works. Join us in our celebration of the women who contribute so much to our communities and to our experiences.

On behalf of the Board and membership of Eastern Edge, I would like to express our gratitude to the writers, who responded with characteristic creativity to the project, to the artists and lenders to the exhibition, to the Newfoundland and Labrador Arts Council for assistance, and to Don Morgan at Killick Press for supporting this publication.

Dionne Snow
Coordinator, Eastern Edge Gallery

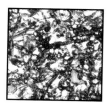

Isobel Brown was born in Glasgow, Scotland and met her Newfoundland husband while they were both serving in the Royal Navy. She came to live in St. John's in 1946. She works in stained glass, copper enamelling, clay, mixed media painting, and lately in chalk drawing. She has written and broadcast commentaries for CBC Radio, and published essays and short stories. Her work in progress is a book about growing up in Glasgow between the two World Wars.

Geraldine Chafe Rubia is the author of *A Poem in My Soup* (Jesperson Press, 1980) and *Skating Among The Graves* (Killick Press, 1991). Her writing has been published in many periodicals and anthologies. Her musical *The Beautity of the Park*, with music by Rubia and by Ed Kavanagh, was performed by students of Random Island Integrated School in the Regional High School Drama Festival 1994 — winning the award for best production of a Newfoundland play. Geraldine Rubia is preparing a new collection of verse.

Isobel Brown

Proud Age, c.1970
clay sculpture, 6½ x 6 x 3 in (16 x 15 x 8 cm)
(photo: Jennifer Morgan)

Isobel Makes Lumps into Rational Documents
On Isobel Brown's clay sculptures:
Proud Age
and Whale Enjoys Man

Isobel

Chaw me a chant
A latter-day chant
A chant that will ken what to say

Respectable Receptacle

What you see
Is all of me
> Alleluia

Fixed dimensions
No intentions
> Alleluia

Nothing hidden
Or forbidden
> Alleluia

Mouldy crumb
Or kingdom come
> Alleluia

Fill me up
I will not sup
> Alleluia

Pass me by
I will not die
> Alleluia

I am at
Your mercy still
> Alleluia

You can smash me
If you will
> Alleluia

Isobel

Blaw me a boast
A brazen-faced boast
A boast that will blaw me away

Old Sam

What a fighter I was!
While others fled
Or fell around me
I struck and took the boldest blows
Prevailed with highest honour

What a life it was!
To wield my swords
To dip my pen
To blazon my words
To keep the faith

What a twist it is!
The hard-earned stipend
Will not meet
One's modest need
In time of peace

How honoured you are!
How grateful
To offer from your plenty
A small salute
To venerable age

Isobel

Fling me a frolic
A lolloping frolic
A frolic that captures the day

WhaleBaby

Free as can be in the walloping sea
Only mother is bigger than me
I lurk or I leap as angishores gaze
For the flick of a fluke in the briny haze
Golloping tidbits wherever I can
Herring or capelin or gingerbread man

Yo Ho for the life I savour
Yo Ho for freedom's flavour
Yo Ho for every blessed saviour
Yo Ho Ho Ho Ho

Rocked in the lap of the billowy deep
Drifting off in a slumbery sleep
Thanking Neptune I'm not a cod
Or a hake or a halibut — Glory to God
Here comes a delicate appetizer
Down the hatch Jack and good-bye to Lizer

Yo Ho for the life I savour
Yo Ho for freedom's flavour
Yo Ho for every blessed saviour
Yo Ho Ho Ho Ho

Isobel

Unloose a lament
A streaming lament
A lament that goes keening astray

JackJonah

Go warn em in Nineveh He says
but I wanted none of it
so what does He do
but cast me into the sea
where He has this girt fish hove to
waitin to swally me up
down in his belly
I bawls out to the Skipper
for three days runnin
till He gets the whale
or whatever it is
to spit me up on the dry land

So what can I do after that
but head out to goddam Nineveh
none of em so much as says Boo
but starts beatin their breasts
and callin for sackcloth and ashes
but that's another story

What I wants to know is
where will it all end
I'm right pissed off
gettin swallied and upchucked
swallied and upchucked
every hundred years or so
till I don't know where I'm at...
> *Lord, I am cast out of thy sight*
> *yet I will look again toward...*
BACCALIEU for godsake!
Shag this
(He takes the whale all by the tail
and turns her inside out)

Whale Enjoys Man, c.1970
clay sculpture, 5½ x 6 x 4 in (14 x 15 x 11 cm)
(photo: Jennifer Morgan)

Holus Bolus

Yo Ho Yo Hoo
We pay our due
There's no one else to save us
Yo Ho Yo Hoo
We love you too
For everything you gave us

We know we are the ocean
We know we are the sky
We are the clay that has its say
We live until we die

Yo Ho Yo Hoo
We pay our due
There's no one else to save us
Yo Ho Yo Hoo
We love you too
For everything you gave us

We know to reap the ocean
We know to clean the sky
We take our pick of stone and stick
We live until we die

Yo Ho Yo Hoo
We pay our due
There's no one else to save us
Yo Ho Yo Hoo
We love you too
For everything you gave us

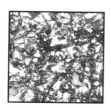

Marlene Creates lives in St. John's, Newfoundland. She was born in Montreal in 1952 and studied visual arts at Queen's University in Kingston, Ontario. She lived in Ottawa for twelve years before moving to Newfoundland — the home of her maternal ancestors — in 1985. Since the 1970s her work has been presented in over one hundred solo and group exhibitions across Canada and in Ireland, Scotland, England, France, and the USA. She has also been the curator of several exhibitions, worked in artist-run centres, and taught visual arts at the University of Ottawa and Algonquin College. Her artistic practice — investigating the relationship between human experience, memory, and the land — has taken her to work in many locations throughout Canada and Britain. Her work is in numerous public collections including the National Gallery of Canada and the Canadian Museum of Contemporary Photography.

Carmelita McGrath is a poet, fiction writer, editor and reviewer. She was born in Branch, St. Mary's Bay and now lives in St. John's. Her books are *Poems on Land and on Water* (Killick Press, 1992) and *Walking to Shenak* (fiction, Killick Press, 1994). She has worked extensively as an editor, most recently as co-editor of *Their Lives and Times, Women in Newfoundland and Labrador, a collage* (Killick Press, 1995). Her poetry, fiction and reviews have appeared in a variety of publications including *TickleAce, Event, The Fiddlehead, The New Quarterly, Poetry Canada, Room of One's Own, The Journey Prize Anthology* and *Books in Canada*.

Marlene Creates

BOG LIMIT
from the series *Language and Land Use, Newfoundland 1994*
assemblage of 3 black & white photographs, selenium-toned silver prints, 16 x 20
in (41 x 51 cm) each, hand written panel, pencil on matboard, 10 x 12 in (25 x 30
cm), and red carnations, framed
16 x 20 in (41 x 51 cm)
(installation photo: Ned Pratt)

opposite page: excerpts

"Is this the park right here?" I heard the man ask. He was operating the loader and filling in the bog with crushed stone. "I thought it was over there. I didn't know this was the park," he said to the man who drove the roller to compress and flatten it out. "What are these flowers doing here?" he asked me. Red carnations lay scattered on the disturbed earth. They had been placed on the construction equipment yesterday by protesters hoping to stop the building of a highway through the park. "The people opposing this road are the hikers and so on," said the man driving the wood loader who joined the conversation from high up in the cab of his truck, "people who have time to hike and time to protest. You take a man who is working seventy or eighty hours a week to raise his family, he hasn't got time for that. The people who want this road don't have time to protest for it."

GRUBBING LIMIT
from the series *Language and Land Use, Newfoundland 1994*
assemblage of 3 black & white photographs, selenium-toned silver prints, 16 x 20
in (41 x 51 cm) each, hand written panel, pencil on matboard, 10 x 12 in (25 x 30
cm), and a section of a felled tree
(installation photo: Ned Pratt)

opposite page: excerpts

The man driving the wood loader, packed to capacity with eighteen cords of tree trunks, stopped on his way out of the park.

"What are the pros and cons of the road?" he asked me from the cab of the truck. "I never put any thought to it," he said. "You'll see," the man driving the roller said to me, "the road will look really nice when it's all finished, when the grass is all planted." A young man arrived, wearing a cap with a Newfoundland and Labrador Forestry badge on it. He was looking for work as a cutter. When the man driving the roller first saw me approach, he had called out to me, "Do you want a job?" When I returned home, I noticed in the newspaper that it was Tree Awareness Day.

Carmelita McGrath

If the Land Has Memory

1. 2015, the Ring Road

Twenty years after you were disturbed
from a long earth-slumber,
cut, compressed, flattened,
your back going hard under burdens—
the hardened shell, rush-hour tonnage, a cacophony
of hurried voices cased in metal

twice a day amid a strange silence,
lull in the hurry-storm—
twenty years later the hard shell of you
gives way again.

*This route is simply too expensive; we cannot keep it
up. The economy being the way it is. Experts assure us
we can build a new road for less. Where? There is nothing
there right now, empty land, used for nothing—
nothing there now but bushes, a few birds, grass and bog, nothing
that couldn't profit from a little landscaping; there is nothing
to prevent us from making a fine road there.*

your old back straightens; you cannot remember
what you were before the road,
but this new deformity stirs with life—
toadflax and iris; dragonfly nymph.

2. On the nature of bogs and wastelands...

They were limitless.
In my childhood, abyssal,
bottomless:
o the crackling bog
o the quaking bog
o the rattling bog

north-atlantic quicksand;

as children we knew
the deep distinction: call it a marsh
and pick berries on it; call it a bog

14

and you'd better watch out.

Bogs swallowed horses, their legs broken,
their high whinnying terror echoing through the night.
Berry-pickers, strayed, disoriented, were lost, the glint
of their buckets gone in the dark: how else to explain
the disappeared? Old Nick used bogs, too much a convenience
for an opportunist to resist; he snapped fingers
laced with flint, drew sparks, and travellers followed,
lured by a miasma of light.

3. 1932: hands were tools, and a boy builds a road

There were too many mouths to feed
and time
had run out for the charms
of readers and sums and schoolyard afternoons

and the boy on the work crew is pulling
out stumps; he and his father, a pick,
a shovel between them, and four hands. Those hands,
eleven years old, were already losing the memory
of the slim shape of a pencil, and his back
was already stiffening into the back of a hard man.

They laid the road, palimpsest
on a hundred-year-old path, on high ground,
creating a road that curved and wound, skirting
wetlands, over which (everyone knew) no road
could be built.

The foreman said they couldn't pay the boy, my father,
as much as the men. His hands were, after all,
small tools lately out of games—but if he worked hard
there was a promise
of half what any man got. Building the road,
the boy turned into a man; even now
he will look at landscapes, say, *You wouldn't put
a house over there; that's not a good spot for a garden.*

He is of the old ways, when the land
suggested something:

look, those great stones (but) in the wrong place
might be a beach
for drying fish, or a wall
to keep something in or something out, or name a space;
a soft depression on a hillside fills with sun and catches
a farmer's eye, shows him a place
to deposit humus where it will hold:

the land was a body of many parts, each
telling a story of its use.

4. On the suspension of disbelief...

What kind of dreamer would you be

if you could walk into a woods, a bogland,
and see four lanes of traffic? Or step,
in late afternoon, into a cathedral of trees
and see a golf course, a man raising a glass of Jamieson's
through a clubhouse window at the ninth hole, which is yet
a white birch. Who would you be, suspended in what dream,

to imagine something more useful than what's there to be seen?

Yet you might dismiss tales of little people, spirit paths,
will-o-the-wisps, strange music, lights in the grass. And
all the while see what is not there, call it *planning*,

castles in the air,
golf courses in the trees,
new roads all leading to our very own Rome,

what kind of dreamer could you be?

5. A hundred years down the road, an old road remembers...

how beautiful this new green grass, how bright!

the words in currency at the time were

you can't stop progress,
people need jobs,
and
effectiveness and efficiency

so what's changed? not much, but dreams displace,
move on to new spaces

sure,
there was protest: red carnations, petals
on scarred earth, reminiscent
of the geography of graves
but
resistance is a hothouse flower itself, needs
constant nurturing in a cold climate

i am wind and sky, bird and wetland
rock and scree, scrub and tree,

have heard all those high voices
sharp, sped up by their very brevity,
one chimes, *you can't stop progress*; another
calls, *yes, but think for a minute, what is it?*

the members of this chorus are constantly being replaced;
they burn bright and briefly

i bear testimony; over my body,
overlay on overlay, are mapped their dreams
and crossings: bell towers
poke out of hummocks, and grass sprouts through the floors
of forgotten houses; under it all
an old story
whose elements never change

i am wind and sky, bird and wetland
rock and scree, scrub and tree.

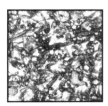 **Kathleen Leah Knowling** was born in St. John's and went to school there and in Canada. She received a degree in history from Columbia University. She has been active in the visual arts for thirty years and has exhibited in Newfoundland, Canada and the United States. Her work is in several collections including the Canada Council Art Bank, the Department of Foreign Affairs, Imperial Oil, Government of Newfoundland and Labrador, Memorial University, and in private collections in Newfoundland, Canada, the United Kingdom and the United States.

Anne Hart is the author of a number of short stories and poems. Her two books of fictional biography, *The Life and Times of Miss Jane Marple* and *The Life and Times of Hercule Poirot*, have been published in North America and Great Britain in hard cover and paperback and translated into five languages. She is head of the Centre for Newfoundland Studies at Memorial University Library.

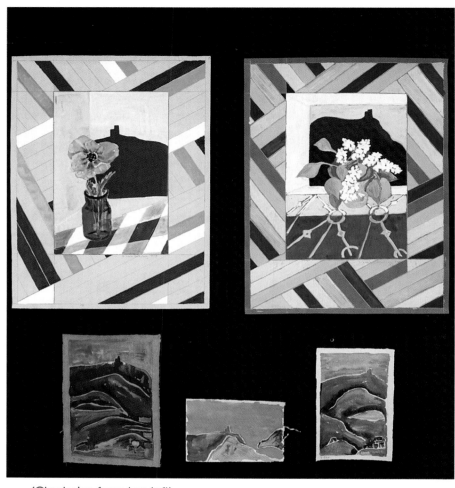

(Clockwise from top left)
Signal Hill With Poppy, 1990-91
mixed media on paper, 25 x 19 in (63.5 x 48 cm)
Signal Hill With White Lilac, 1990
mixed media on paper, 25½ x 19½ in (65 x 49.5 cm)
Signal Hill, Orange Sky, 1992
gouache on paper, 11¼ x 7½ in (28.5 x 19 cm)
Signal Hill, Red Outline, 1992
gouache on paper, 6¼ x 9½ in (16 x 24 cm)
Signal Hill With Houses, 1992
gouache on paper, 13 x 9¾ in (33 x 25 cm)
(photo: Ned Pratt)

"I remember as a girl returning to St. John's after a long absence and realizing that it was here that I wanted to spend my life. Signal Hill, in particular, is always a reminder and metaphor of this decision. I have sketched and painted it hundreds, perhaps thousands, of times."

— Kathleen (Muffet) Knowling

not just any spell

in a far distant land
Muffet runs through Senior
Hall straight down Sunny Run
through Prefects' Porch & jumps
into a trunk marked HOME
days later her ship is
sighted from a magic
tower high atop a
chameleon hill & when
the cannon booms above
the Narrows Muffet knows
she's made it safe & sound
what feasting what dancing
but all the while in the
Waterford River a
Mermaid is waiting no
one has seen this Mermaid
since R. Whitbourne in sixteen
ten but here comes Muffet
walking off the feasting
splash ah my darling says
the Mermaid you think no
ransom is owing for
such joy well here's your spell
see the chameleon
hill that guards our city
from this day on your fate
will be to ever paint
her portrait still life wild
life sun nude storm friezed
monotone polychrome
chiaroscuro &
splash her discourse done the
Mermaid disappears &
Muffet ever after charmed
begins that very day
her artful thraldom's task

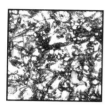

Debra Kuzyk was born and raised in Saskatchewan. She graduated with a degree in Education from the University of Saskatchewan before attending the Nova Scotia College of Art and Design in Halifax. Once she received her degree in fine art in 1983, she moved to Stephenville, Newfoundland to teach art to high school students. Between then and now she has had numerous experiences which have influenced her life and her art. Outstanding among them were the times spent in India, Africa and Central America. She divides her time between creating works of art, producing functional pottery, and spending time with her family and new baby, Lillian Pearl.

Lisa Moore is a St. John's writer. She graduated from the Nova Scotia College of Art and Design and is the author of *Degrees of Nakedness*, a collection of short stories. She is presently spending her time with a family who laughs a lot, bringing home the butter, and writing a novel.

Debra Kuzyk

Valentine, 1994, mixed media
13½ in (34 cm) diameter
collection: Ray Mackie
(photo: Ned Pratt)

Four Valentines

The first valentine

We couldn't sleep on the bus. Or hardly. Then it broke down. Stuck there on the side of the highway between Toronto and Ottawa. You didn't sleep at all. I woke to see a blazing sun dripping down the window like a tablespoon of honey but red and showing all the hairline scratches in the plexiglass. You came home at four-thirty the night before, out carousing with your buddies. Kicked in a t.v. under a magnolia tree. And the bang, you said. I wake in a strange bed not knowing who's coming through the door or where I am until I hear the rip of the velcro flaps on your sneakers.

Couldn't you have gotten glass in your face? I touch your cheek with the back of my finger.

It imploded, you say and fall asleep with your arm flung across the pillow.

I get my hair cut just before we get on the bus and you can't keep your hands off the back of my neck.

You say, I love your neck.

What about the rest of me?

Just your neck.

The gay couple opposite us sleeping, folding knees and elbows together elegantly, like origami, one man with a head of gold curls that catches the red rays, a grass fire, his lover's hand bent over his head like a weeping willow. Murmurs. The air conditioning numbing my bare legs.

In Ottawa at six a.m. a heatwave that's closing schools. I wash my hair in the bathroom. Even the cold water is lukewarm. Tuck our luggage into a locker, the fecund puff of breath from the plastic bag of softening mangoes. Empty streets except a paving truck spuming glittery chunks of rock out a metal snout. And the stink of tar like wads of velvet in the throat. We have been twenty-four hours without sleep. Another eight before the plane leaves. Finally, outside the bus station, we sit on an island of grass about as big as two parked cars. We have nowhere else to wait. You sleep with your head in my lap. And you ask with your eyes still closed, Will you make love in those bushes over there?

The steel side of a bus roaring past, sun flanked. The chainlink shadow of the fence shifting on your thigh.

And we get up and go into some stores. You hold my neck while you purchase small toys for Rose, rose-tinted glasses, a cigarette that squirts water.

We pass a boy with a broom trying to knock something from the branches of a small tree in the concrete planter. We look up into the starry dark tree. The handle of the broom like the wand of a metronome marking a dirge. You take the broom. The handle sways, the earth tips, a baseball hits the sidewalk like a stone.

Just moments before the plane touches down in Newfoundland eight hours later and you have your shoulder and head squashed against the glass to see everything — you always take the window seat — you turn to me and say, Lisa, I was just wondering, was there any chance this morning that you would have gone into those bushes with me, because I had the feeling at the time, because I was half asleep, and the heat wave, and that t.v. imploding, I had the feeling you were really close to doing it.

I say, Steve, there were no bushes.

The second valentine

This is Marrakesh, on our honeymoon. And the two Moroccan sisters we meet say, Your honeymoon? But you must have a Moroccan wedding.

They dress me in a long white robe and white slippers with pointed toes and embroidered with gold thread. They each take one of my hands and lead me out into the dusk. I look back over my shoulder at you and they laugh.

You will see him again, don't worry.

Down a labyrinth of narrow streets at dusk with motorcycles and bicycles bending around us and plumes of dust. They knock on a thick wooden door with iron studs and it swings open. A Turkish bath. They tell me to take off my clothes, everything. Inside, the room is full of steam and naked women. These women, all of them, have long wet black hair streaming down their backs. Blue-black hair to the small of the back and even longer. A lot of them are pregnant, and they are laughing and talking and pouring buckets of water over each other so that the long black hair parts at the neck and falls over both shoulders under the weight of the falling water. There are squares of blue glass embedded in the stone walls. Blue bands of light crisscross all over the room like a fishing net snagging the slow rising steam. Both the sisters, Rashida and Nasha, pour buckets of very hot water over me and they scrub me. They scrub every inch of my skin with a rough cloth. Later, when we get back to their house, they dress me in traditional Moroccan wedding clothes. They have a lot of gold jewellery. A gold chain with jewels on my forehead. So many necklaces they begin to weigh on my chest. Dark gold. Honey gold. The weight of it. And then a crown snug on my temples. And a veil, heavily embroidered. They pin the back of the veil to the wall with thumb tacks. Now I can't move my head.

Where is Steve? I ask Rashida.

Don't move your lips, she says. She's putting on my lipstick.

Nasha takes several strings of Christmas mini-lights from a suitcase. She puts them around my neck, in the points of the crown, along my forehead. She plugs them in and they are the blinking kind.

There will be tea soon, she says.

Rashida says, My mother does this for her village, dresses all the brides. These jewels have been passed down from my great-grandmother and before her.

They stand back for a moment and look at me. Then Rashida knocks on the door.

You come in wearing a simple flowing white gown. When you see me you are shocked.

Lisa?

Rashida says, *Now* you are married.

The third valentine

You are very excited. You and Mark Brown and Ted Ross are dressing up as women. Your sister Susan is going. She's wearing my black vinyl hotpants and a wimple and veil. I'm working. I can't go. You phone me at work. You say, Where are your fishnet stockings?

You say, I can't talk now, I have to get ready. This is going to be some party.

I hang up. I sit by the phone. I phone you back. There's laughter in the kitchen. A pause before you say hello.

I say, What's so funny there?

Hello.

What's going on?

You say, Ted Ross makes one hell of an ugly woman. You should see him, Lisa. We have to go now, our ride is waiting. You should see Susan.

There are whoops and catcalls in the background.

You say, I have to go baby.

I'm taking care of two teenagers, but they are out for the evening. I have to stay awake until they get home. I flick through the channels. Lady Jane Grey getting beheaded. There's a party going on in the next apartment. When I lean against the wall I can feel the pounding music in my shoulder. The heat is down low and I'm getting a fever. I make a cup of tea and look out the window. There's a row of brick apartments across the street. A scarecrow in a plaid shirt and overalls sitting on a lawn chair, a wide-brimmed hat pulled down over his face, a pumpkin at his feet. The scarecrow has been there for three weeks. On Halloween night the owner of the house dresses in the same costume, sits in the lawnchair with the brim pulled down over his eyes and when the neighbourhood kids approach the doorbell he leaps up and yells Booo.

At one-thirty the teenagers phone. They aren't coming home. I'm free to leave. It will be an expensive taxi ride. I won't get to the party until about two.

I squeeze the white paint from a tube onto my fingers and smear it on my face. I look at myself. It makes the curve of my bones more visible. I smile. My teeth and eyeballs look yellowish against the pure white. My eyelids reddish. I get an old black felt hat, tuck up my hair. A long black cloak. Two red circles on my cheeks with lipstick. Dark red lips. Mascara.

Two-thirty when I get to the party. Susan is sitting at the dining room table. I sit on the empty chair beside her.

She says, Hello.

I look into her eyes. We are sitting like that and she looks at me. She doesn't know who I am. There is a moment of hesitation when she lifts her beer bottle. She takes a long sip. A hesitation, as though it is coming to her who I am. But it does not come to her. She believes I am at work. She puts the beer bottle on the table.

She says, How are you?

Fine.

Even with my voice she doesn't know.

I say, How are you?

She clutches my arm and says, Jesus! What are you doing here?

The girls aren't coming home, I was free to leave.

She says, You're here!

Yes. Where's Steve? Is he here?

He's dancing. In the rec room.

And there beside Susan, Ted Ross. His rugby shoulders in pink polyester ruffles. His grey wig askew. He fingers a loop of pearls. I get up to find you. You are coming up the stairs from the rec room and I put both my arms out and block the way. You're wearing my elastic mini-dress with the orange, turquoise, red, and yellow flowers. Fishnet stockings. Breasts. A long black wig. You flick a strand over your shoulder. You are drunk and a film of sweat makes your mascara smudge. Hot from dancing.

You say, Excuse me. I don't move.

Pardon me.

And then you see I'm not moving and you look straight into my eyes. Sway a little and you smile. We are very close. I feel your breath on my face.

You say carefully, I wonder, would you mind moving out of my way.

I am looking into your eyes, and we have been married eight years and you are looking into my eyes. My heart is beating like crazy. I put my hand on your crotch.

And you don't move. We stand like that.

You say, Who are you?

I lean forward and kiss you. I just let my tongue barely touch your tongue, and my hand still on your crotch.

And you say, I know you! You're Lisa Moore.

The fourth valentine

Then the bus stop. The bus stop in front of the Village the day after Earl and Martina's wedding. And I am trying to read Heraclitus because you wrote your thesis on him. There at the bus stop. Wind snappity in the plastic shopping bags. A woman in a long silver dress, crepuscular light. Pewter pouring over her thighs, pooling at her ankle, hip. She turns her head and the wind lifts her hair.

A drunk man with one angry tooth in his bottom jaw says, Give me that book.

I hand him the book with the stone bust of Heraclitus on the cover. There are women lined up all down the benches. Women with big broad chests hanging most of the way down their bellies.

The man holds the book at arm's length and squints at it.

That's when they knew how to make men, he says.

He taps Heraclitus on the stone cheek, They knew what it took back then. He holds the book up for everyone at the bus stop to see.

He says, I'm waiting for route eight.

One of the women at the end of the bench asks him with disgust, Can you read? Try reading that schedule on the wall.

He says, I don't need no schedule, I know how to chart my course by the stars. I know a thing or two this crowd has forgotten.

Well you'll be here when the stars come out then, because route eight is discontinued.

There's no route eight, another woman says.

He squints at each of the women and takes a cigarette out of his pocket. He lights it and looks out over the parking lot.

He says, I'll sing now. I'll sing for you.

He leans over the garbage bin, mustard-smeared napkins hanging out the maw, tucks the cigarette into the curl of his hand and everyone turns away from him. The women are united in the grim agreement that they will not indulge him. They look at the parking lot, at the sky, the traffic, but listen as he sings,

And how I wish for those fine days
to come a-ga-in once more,
but come again they never will
cause now I'm sixty-four.

I think about Earl and Martina getting married in Bannerman Park and she turned to him and said, Earl, you are the kindest man I ever met.

How it boils down to that, kindness. I want to be sixty-four with you Steve. A hard gust of wind hits the glass walls with rain, the beads driven sideways. Three teenage girls rush in from outside, giggling. Over Mount Pearl, lightning.

The old man says, I'll never see sixty-four again, and neither will he. Handing me the Heraclitus.

At the wedding reception Martina threw the bouquet. She was sitting on a chair in the middle of the emptied dance floor, red and blue spotlights spilling over the walls, the crowd, her ivory lace wedding dress. Striptease music, her head thrown back in laughter. Her legs spread wide and feet planted and the groom with a beer in each hand. He weaves toward her and kneels between her legs. Gently, for a long time, he reaches up under her dress and finally retrieves the garter, face flushed. He hands it to her and she slaps his face with it twice and tucks it down the front of her dress. She grabs his head in her hands, pulls his face to her breasts. And they stay like that for a long time.

The old man stops singing and sits on the bench beside me.

He says, You're looking pretty good.

I say, Not so bad yourself.

There's a flake of tobacco on his lip.

I see you're a married woman, he says, looking at my hand.

Yes I am.

But seriously, he says, you must have considered having an affair. My God, the same man for how many years?

Eight years, I say. The women down the bench are listening carefully.

I say, But I never sleep with the same man twice.

You don't?

It's like Heraclitus says, No man ever steps in the same river twice.

(Sometimes I get into bed with you Steve and I hold your face in my hands and I say to myself, What do I know about you for sure? What do I know, absolutely? And then I imagine that you might open your mouth and speak Polish. You are always someone different. Love is like a sawblade through the chestbone. You must always be open. Alert. It could be Polish.)

The old guy says, Well, I'm never the same man twice either. And he burps.

A woman on the bench says, Jesus, route eight is hauling up.

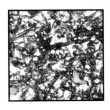

Bonnie Leyton apprenticed and worked as a potter first in England, then in Ontario and Newfoundland, where she studied fine art and sculpture at Memorial University's Department of Continuing Studies. She works primarily in clay but uses any appropriate materials to express her ideas. A sense of place, where we fit into the world, and how the world fits around us: these are the themes she constantly explores. Her works are in private and public collections. She co-ordinated *Land and Sea: Eight Artists From Newfoundland*, an exhibition that is currently travelling in Ireland, and she is co-curating an exhibition of Irish art which will travel to Canada. She has served on many art boards and is presently chair of the board of Eastern Edge Gallery.

Lillian Bouzane is a poet who also writes short stories and essays. She has two books of poetry — *Back to Back* (with Harold Paddock) and *Point Blank* (with Grace Butt). Her suite of poems "In the Time of Wolves" was made into a docu-drama by CBC (1992) and won two international awards — The Gabriel and The New York Festival Award; this work was also nominated for a Peabody. "In the Time of Wolves" was first published in TickleAce No. 29 in 1995. She won first place in the Arts and Letters Competition's Non-Fictional Prose Category (1994), and her essay "The Whittler" was short-listed for a Tilden Canadian Literary Award (1995).

Bonnie Leyton

Stoneware Bowl, 1995
stoneware clay and glaze with gold lustre, 13 x 2½ in (33 x 6 cm)
(photo: Ned Pratt)

The Bowl

The bowl was large. It was a gift. It had a deep chocolate glaze. It could hold a dozen and a half delicious reds. It stood on the counter and held the day's fruit: apples, oranges, bananas and, in season, a persimmon or two. In my white and wheat coloured kitchen it caught the eye.

Its full lustre was on display, however, only on the occasion of Halloween, when I filled it with apples and placed it on the floor under the light in the front hall and waited for the bell to ring.

As I opened the door to the first goblin of the night, the light over the door and the light in the hall streamed together and produced dancing stars on the glaze of the chocolate rim and they, in turn, bounced off the gleam and glimmer of the apples; the goblins—dazzled—squealed with delight.

As the children came and went, I found myself waiting for the uncovering of the aubergine waterfall that started at the rim of the bowl and circled half way around and down the inner side. The last few apples picked off the bottom uncovered the creamy froth stippled in spray and foam.

I often wondered why in all the years I owned the bowl I didn't give it its proper place on the floor in the living room, or in my study, for it was only when it was empty and I looked down into it, did the midnight waterfall that cascaded its inner side guide my eye to the burst of spray at the bottom. It never ceased to delight.

The last Halloween I owned the bowl, more children came to the door than usual, and I had refilled it a number of times. Finally, the bell fell silent, and I was standing contemplating the design and sheen when a ripple around the rim, that I hadn't noticed before, caught my attention. I was standing there in that forgetfulness of self and surroundings that an object so lovely instills when my father came up behind me on his slippered feet; I was startled by his question.

What do you see?

I believe that ridge at the lip of the bowl might have been made by the thumb of the potter.

My father bent, picked up the bowl, put it in the crook of his arm, and traced his thumb around the ridge.

Yes, I think you're right.

I have been given other pieces of pottery over the years, and some that stand here and there in my house I have purchased, but it's the bowl: the high gloss of its chocolate sides, its aubergine waterfall, the spray rising at the bottom, and the signature of the potter's thumb, that I remember on a day.

Bonnie Leyton

It's a Mystery to Me, 1990,
clay, wood and acrylic paint, 15½ x 17 x 17 in (39 x 43 x 43 cm),
courtesy of Emma Butler Gallery
(photo: Ned Pratt)

Lillian Bouzane

In the Time of Wolves

David Day (Council to the Royal Commission on Sexual and Physical Abuse at Mount Cashel Orphanage) said...he believes the investigation may reach as far back as the 1950s. (Evening Telegram, *16 July 1989*)

They have flung open the gates to the sheepfold
They have flung them open long ago
And the lambs long ago have shattered in the raging storm
The glass of their broken lives glitters in the abandoned sheepfold
Their down falling sighs could founder Rome

A former resident of Mount Cashel Boys Home (operated by the Irish Christian Brothers) says he ran away because of sexual and physical abuse, but he was returned to the same person at the home who abused him despite his pleas to the Police and Social Workers. (Evening Telegram, *12 Nov. 1989*)

Sir, is there no one to take me off the hooks?
Night after night after night the Brother sticks his tongue in my mouth.
Night after night after night he sticks his finger up my bum.
Night after night after night he beats my little brother.
Night after night after night I count the welts on my body.
Night after night after night I watch as he marauds through the dorm
For the love of Christ Sir, take us off the hooks.

When I saw the marks on their bodies
I went to the Government
I went to the Church
I went to the Police
I went to the Press
    They questioned my sanity
    They threatened me with their best lawyers
    They sat with eyes of flint
        As a mother knows, I knew
        They would sacrifice every last child
        To their will, to their wolfish want
        I knew they knew with absolute assurance
        The law was their mother — their father
        That they would get away with it — forever

Where under the sun is the comforter
    To steady the tremble of my hands
    To rest the tremor of my heart
    To give me nights of untroubled sleep

Where under the sun is the counsellor to take
    The panic from my eyes
    The cry from my mouth
    The jump from my nerves

Where under the sun can I go that
    My body will not remember the blows
    My ears will not hear the curses
    My dreams will not betray me into hell

Mrs. Baird said she had no idea when she signed her sons into the Orphanage they stood to be subjects of physical or sexual abuse. "If I had any idea that was going on, when I went in for the boys I would have gone with a baseball bat." (Evening Telegram, 31 Oct. 1989)

As God is my Judge I want those Brothers who raped my children
to come up against the Justice of God — and soon.
I want blackness to enter their minds and their legs to come out
from under them.
I want their work to turn to ashes in their mouths.
I want sweet sleep to abandon them.
I want their eyes never again to close on a peaceful night.
I want them ever to be in fear of the loss of Heaven and be given
visions of Hell.
I want remorse to visit their minds and finally their hearts to be broken.
I want them to beg forgiveness from my children, on their knees,
in sackcloth.
I want the cost of their souls to hang on this action.
I want the fire of the justice of God to be wrapped round their shoulders
and I want to witness it.
As God is my Judge,
                    I want my prayers answered.

I WAS HOLY MOTHER CHURCH

I entered the monastery
to carry that most ancient power
on my not insignificant shoulders;
they gave me fifty orphans,
the dirt of the world,
other dirty men's dirty sperm;
I resented it.

Why wouldn't I take what I wanted?
Who could touch me?
    I was Holy Mother Church
    and every scarlet prelate
    pockets stuffed with
        lawyers
        magistrates
        whole governments
            would be my Mother
            my Father
            my Judge
            my Jury.

    Molest a few orphans?
    The flight path to the top!

        i took it.
            I took it.
            I TOOK IT.

Brother Gabriel McHugh (Superior General of the Congrega-
tion of the Irish Christian Brothers) called from Rome to
appear before The Commission said he made no requests to
Vincent McCarthy (Deputy Minister of Justice) or the De-
partment of Social Services to have psychological assistance
provided for the boys who had allegedly been assaulted. (Sunday Express, *15 Dec. 1989*)

To give up Rome
The cool morning walks among the ruins
The Summer Place in the Tuscan Hills
The summons to lunch with the Pope
The occasional dinner with the Augustinians
The wine cellar full of Amontillado
      For a few orphans
      It's a thought not to be clung to
            I have hired the best counsel
            I have presented myself to The Commission
            I have wrapped myself in the cloth

            I have not budged from my story
            I will have my way

MOTHER OF THE CONDEMNED

I dressed him in velvet
I sent him to the best schools
I took the lives of his sisters and put them to his service
I made a path for him through the house
I did without for his pleasure
When he entered the Church I thanked God on my knees
When he supervised the Orphanage I wrapped him in light
When he was hailed into court I carried a spike in my heart
When he was condemned I wished he never was born

THE ARCHBISHOP

I banked on the boy not talking

I banked on the mother not talking

I banked on the people not talking

I banked on the judge not talking

I banked on the social worker not talking

I banked on the secretary not talking

> My mitre
> My cope
> My staff
> My ring

> I banked on them to cover me

> I banked on them

THE DEMONS HAVE BEEN UNCOUPLED

Listen to me
Hold up your heads
You who, even in your cots, were snuffled by wolves
The demons have been uncoupled
One by one by one they have been thrown down
They cringe in the jails of the land
They pace with the grit of their fall in their teeth
Hold up your heads
Listen to me

> You have been observed by eyes brighter than the stars

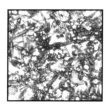

Jennifer Morgan has a certificate in Graphic Arts from The College of Trades and Technology in St. John's and a Bachelor of Arts in Art and Theology from Andrews University, Michigan. She has illustrated four books produced by Newfoundland publishers. Aside from two Arts and Letters Competition exhibitions, this is the first time her work has been exhibited. In 1989, at Williams Lake, B.C., she burned all but one of her previous paintings. She considers that bonfire the best contribution she has made thus far to Canadian art.

Bernice Morgan has been writing since the 1950s. Her short stories have been published in literary magazines, anthologies and textbooks, including the book *Cultures*, recently published by Harcourt Brace. She is the author of two novels published by Breakwater, *Random Passage* in 1992 and *Waiting for Time* in 1994. Her most recent novel received both The Canadian Authors Association Award for Fiction and The Thomas H. Raddall Atlantic Fiction Award.

Jennifer Morgan

Footwashing, 1995
acrylic on stretched canvas,5 x 4 ft (1.5 x 1.2 m)
(photo: Jennifer Morgan)

Bernice Morgan

Footwashing

Although the incentive for this combination of art and writing came from artists, I sense a certain uneasiness on their part with the idea of words being imposed upon image — the same unease I would feel with idea of image being imposed upon words. In the case of Jennifer Morgan and myself this discomfort may go deeper, not just because of our family relationship and our common association with Jennifer's subject matter, but also, perhaps mainly, because her Coley's Point series is a work-in-progress. The artist knows that words can flatten images, stratifying them into one time and one place. She is right of course, art should be different for each viewer and different each time viewed.

Because of this my reflections on Jennifer's art come with a disclaimer: "What follows is a work of fiction, the product of one writer's imagination at one moment in time. Any resemblance between these words and the images you see at this moment is entirely coincidental."

The house in Coley's Point was built in 1866 by a young fisherman named Abraham Morgan for his bride Rachel. In 1887, when their fifteen-year-old son almost drowned on the Labrador, Rachel vowed that no man in her family would ever again make his living on the sea. After that, Abraham worked in St. John's for nine months of the year, returning at Christmas to Coley's Point where Rachel and her daughters kept gardens, goats and hens.

In 1929 Rachel and Abraham's grandson and his bride spent their honeymoon in the house with Lizzie, the strange aunt who lived there alone for years and years.

After Lizzie's death the house became an in-between place, a sometimes place: haven for a soldier wanting peace and quiet, refuge for a university teacher gone deaf in mid-career, a popular destination for Sunday afternoon drives, an overnight stop for root-seeking American cousins. One winter it sheltered Coley's Point neighbours whose roof had blown away and one summer a young man who spent the months between high school and university brooding and building fences. The house has been a place in which to hide, to mourn, to celebrate, to berrypick, to dream, a place to sit on mawsy June days waiting for caplin to roll, on Guy Fawkes' Nights watching fires burn around the shore.

Though sagging a little, it is built on rocks and two huge tree trunks, the house stands today much as it did when Abraham brought Rachel to it from Ship Cove. It is a fisherman's house, spare and plain, without cupboards or closets but with a faint bevelled decoration line along the edges of the hand-sawn ceiling beams, thick beams and a low ceiling, for Abraham was not

45

a tall man. The family has never had the inclination to change the house into some Victorian cottage it never was — or the money (as one crass daughter-in-law suggested) to pull it down to build new and further back from the sea.

The descendants of Rachel and Abraham are frugal, little has been thrown away. But, from time to time, haphazardly as need dictates and money permits, things have been added: handmade washstands, mismatched dishes, the large, out-of-place photo of a terribly sad child that hangs just inside the front door, a Bowrings calendar from 1904, the kitchen wall-clock that has not ticked in living memory, odds and ends of furniture unfit for St. John's houses. In the upstairs hall is a bookcase containing The Standard Young Abstainers Recital Book, Practical Domestic Hygiene by Notter and Firth, published in 1907, an 1868 collection of essays on educational reform by Robert H. Quick, late Vicar of Sedbergh, and several London Religious Tract Society's shilling illustrated series of books "specially suited for working people," including *Widow Clark's Home and What Changed It*. Abraham probably built the small bookcase, which has a fold-out desk panel, for his daughter Emma who was born when her parents were in their late forties. Emma became a teacher, her Normal School certificates still hang in the front room. She married well and went to live in Boston.

In the 1930s the young couples brought smart, wooden deck chairs over to the house, electric wiring was installed in the 1940s and a deck (the chairs would never stand upright in the sloping yard) was added in the 1970s. Because there is no counter space, the electric kettle, itself a relic, usually sits on the black unlit stove above which hangs the framed plaque one of Rachel's sons bought in Halifax. "What Is Home Without A Mother" the scrolled, flower-bedecked letters ask — there is no question mark. To one side of the stove, a white microwave oven sits on a special shelf constructed by Abraham's great-grandson.

Generations of children have added their own layers of detritus to the house. A set of horse's teeth grin down from the back porch window ledge, nearby is a Baden Powell cookie tin, a new flashlight and a plastic sand-bucket containing one seagull feather. In a corner of the front room are a few board games, tattered ten-cent comics, half-used colouring books.

Things from outside come inside. Hidey-holes contain bits of rusting iron, dried starfish, driftwood, shells and pine cones. This summer a new grandchild brought in a basket of small white stones from the beach.

On the back of a program guide for The Art Gallery of Ontario I have scrawled, "Recasting symbols in new roles and establishing new relationships between them is the essence of twentieth century post-modernism."

This quotation, copied down at a gallery lecture, is not just part of my ongoing, and possibly futile, desire to understand post-modernism; it reminded me of something—something I glimpsed in Jennifer's early sketches of Coley's Point and see again in these large paintings of the old house.

In these pictures I feel the artist's desire to somehow capture a sense of life, space and time — to portray that quality and variety of life that exists in *things* — to reconcile the unreconcilable by showing both the vitality and the terrible fragility of past action. She is depicting time not as a passage from point to point (the writer's way) but as a spiral: endless layers that cross and recross — but not predictably or in any perceivable pattern. Each object in the picture carries not only its own history but accumulates other histories in relation to objects around it and in relation to the history of the viewer.

Although the artist can only depict one moment — the present moment — her work resonates with the past and with the future. Time is evoked here as cyclical, perhaps random. Beyond the glass the cold blue sky will darken, dust will accumulate on the white window ledge, already faded curtains will fade even more. The basin in which Abraham soaked his feet, the same basin strange Lizzie used to gather caplin and feed her hens, may someday become a centrepiece filled with oranges and pine cones, or may be used to wash the grimy faces of children or to pick berries in. Or maybe, if time should last and caplin come back, the basin will again scoop silver fish from the foaming sea — or it may be tossed into the garden to rust away.

We see these objects in an abandoned time. Life has been interrupted, the door has just slammed shut, the key has turned, voices faded, people have gone off down the lane—gone to war, gone to fish, gone to look for work in St. John's or Toronto, gone to live in Barbados or Boston or Vancouver. Maybe they will come back. Maybe not.

No matter. The sea will keep pounding, winters will come and go. The house will freeze and thaw, freeze and thaw. Each spring the tree trunks holding it up will settle a little further into the earth.

And who knows? They may come back. Perhaps in decades, perhaps in seconds someone will walk through the door, toss their belongings onto the couch and light the stove. Perhaps people will again sit around the table, drinking tea, watching the sea, eating pizza, talking or reading the Bible or playing computer games. Children may sing, quarrel, laugh, cry, tell stories, be frightened by the strange child in the hall picture, they may try on the dark dresses now mouldering in an upstairs trunk, dig out their grandmother's dried-up paint brushes, or play chip-chip with the small white stones brought up from the beach years ago by other children.

Perhaps . . .

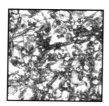 **Rae Perlin** was born in St. John's in 1910. She studied art for a number of years in New York and Paris. She travelled and painted throughout Europe before returning to Newfoundland in 1959. She has been art critic for both *The Daily News* and *The Evening Telegram* and has won many awards. She still lives in St. John's.

Helen Fogwill Porter was born and grew up in St. John's where she still lives. Her publications include *Below the Bridge* (1980), *January, February, June or July* (1988) and *A Long and Lonely Ride* (1991). All were published by Breakwater Books. Her short stories, poetry, essays and reviews have appeared in magazines and anthologies across Canada and overseas.

In the Luxembourg Gardens, 1953
watercolour, 5½ x 8½ in (14 x 21.6 cm), collection: Kathy Porter

Standing Single
Rae Perlin's *In the Luxembourg Gardens*

The woman in the Luxembourg Gardens looks completely at ease with herself. She has a broad backside and has probably borne children. She's not reading, not eating or drinking, not doing anything. Probably not even thinking. I like it that I can't see her face. Or her hands. I'd say this is one of the few times in her life that her hands are empty. She's surrounded by the thick trunks of old trees. High above are the leaves that are perhaps sheltering her from the sun.

Her back is straight but not stiff. Her head does not droop or nod. Her eyes may or may not be closed.

When I look at this painting I think of Rae Perlin in Paris in 1953. She left Newfoundland in 1931 to study nursing in New York City. Such a solid, respectable profession, nursing. A noble calling for a young woman of that time. And Rae became an excellent nurse.

Rae had always loved to draw. Her sketch books went with her everywhere. When she left Bishop Spencer School in St. John's, the headmistress, Miss Cherrington, advised her to go into journalism since "art was a hazardous way to earn a living." But after she got her nursing degree it was art Rae studied in New York, with Samuel Brecher, her "greatest influence."

When Rae moved to Paris in 1950, she continued to use as her models people unknown to her. People she was curious about. In *In the Luxembourg Gardens*, because Rae sketched her subject from behind, the woman didn't know she was being observed. Ever respectful of the privacy of others, Rae took comfort in working unnoticed.

Rae Perlin, who loves company, has spent much of her adult life alone, except for a succession of cats. She knows that being alone doesn't necessarily mean being lonely. Rae has always been strongly connected to the world, and thought of it as a global village long before that term became popular. She uses newspapers, magazines, radio, television, letters and social and professional gatherings to keep herself in touch with what's going on here and elsewhere. Her attachment to the Baha'i faith, which works toward the unity of all religions, has taken her in a different direction. Yet this commitment can be seen as part of a natural progression in a life dedicated to inquiry, analysis and concern for humanity.

Rae's letters to editors, writers, producers, politicians, many of them never sent, would fill a large book. They provide important signposts of what's been going on in the world for the past forty or more years. World leaders would benefit from her wise counsel.

Why do so many of us believe that we can't be happy or fulfilled except in the presence of others? The woman in the Luxembourg Gardens was probably temporarily alone, and pleased to be so. Like one of my fictional characters she could be saying to herself, "Everything, for the moment, is beautifully out of my hands." Isn't it only people whose hands, hearts and minds are usually full who can appreciate this blessed idleness?

In the aptly titled book *Not A Still Life, The Art and Writings of Rae Perlin*, editor Marian Frances White quotes Rae as saying, "My favourite time for reading is at night. I think it's a waste to go to bed with the lovely quiet and light around you and just switch off into the darkness. I can't do that."

For the past twelve years I've been living alone. I often take comfort from Rae's words and images, and from Rae herself, an independent woman all her life. As the American poet Alice Cary (1820-1871) wrote:

"Women and men in a crowd meet and mingle
Yet with itself every soul standeth single."

I believe Rae Perlin has always understood this. Perhaps the woman enjoying her solitude in the Luxembourg Gardens knew it too, and, like Rae, was not daunted.

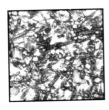

Jennifer Pohl was in the second graduating class from Sir Wilfred Grenfell College School for Fine Art in Corner Brook. In 1993 she received a BFA with the Gold Medal for Excellence in Visual Arts. Half German and three quarters Newfoundlander, She has spent most of her twenty-six years in transit, including a nine-year stint in the English Channel Islands several lifetimes ago. She was awarded a Canada Council Explorations grant for her first solo show *not broken crockery* and has since been involved in several group shows including RCA Visual's *Six Women Present* and the Devon House *Wearable Art* show. In 1995 the artist presented a second solo painting exhibition, *Mother Mary, Wicked Women and Other Stories* at the R.C.A. Visual Gallery. In the same year she was awarded first place in the Senior Painting Division of the Newfoundland and Labrador Arts and Letters Competition. A detail of the winning piece can be seen on the cover of Agnes Walsh's recent book of poetry, *In The Old Country of My Heart.*

Agnes Walsh was born in Placentia, Newfoundland. She has worked in local theatre for seventeen years and in 1995 published her first collection of poems with Killick Press entitled *In The Old Country of My Heart.* She lives in St. John's with her two children, Patrick and Simone.

Jennifer Pohl

Survivors, 1995
oil on canvas, 16½ x 19¾ in (42 x 50 cm)
(photo: Ned Pratt)

Agnes Walsh
for my mother

Patricia and Thomas

The trader anchored in the harbour and the packmen came out on deck. They spread their wares: Gerald S. Doyle products, jewellery, boots, and clothes. Men rowed out standing up. Since it was a short row, to sit down would look too leisurely. Women never went but only hoped the men got right what they wanted.

Tom wasn't sent but he went. He picked out a ring, a thin gold band, paid in coin and rowed back to the creek half-grinning.

Patsy was turning fish in the hot August sun. Her stomach was swelled only slightly, maybe she could get away with it. Anyway, there was Tom rowing towards her looking cocksure and full of purpose. Winter wouldn't be so hard after all.

Margaret

When Aunt Peg came back home she wanted to be called Margaret. I said ah, but I love the sound of Aunt Peg. She pulled back, set her shoulders just so and exhaled sharp and quick through her nostrils. I never said Peg again.

She threw a glassful of beer onto my fifth cousin Anthony's chest, telling him she would not let the Americans be talked about like that. I hear she squared her shoulders, pushed back from the table, went over to my mother's house and changed her airline ticket to get the hell out of Newfoundland and home to Brooklyn.

It irritates my mother to no end that Margaret is so goddamned proud. She won't return. Aunt Lil says she never will. They talk about her in the parlour, I listen from the kitchen. There's more to it than Anthony and the Yanks. That priest on Jude Island who tried to haul her into his bed. She went home, didn't say a word to anyone. He got up at the pulpit the next morning, scared to let another minute pass, and denounced her as a liar who should be tarred and feathered. But she hadn't told a soul, though by then it was too late. No one believed her. Her own mother turned away.

Aunt Margaret came back when Grandmother was in the ground. Proud and fierce she walked through our town butting invisible enemies. I became her silent bodyguard. I wanted her honoured here... but too late, too late, it was far too late.

Now she'll never come back.

She'll be buried in Brooklyn, New York.

Sisley

The family says, "Well sure everyone knows Sis is an alcoholic. She can't get herself to bed without staggering, would get lost if she had to follow a straight line."

Sisley came home once but I never saw her. "Mom, how come I never met Aunt Sis?"

"Your Aunt Sis? I'll tell you why. Because she landed into town, went to Jimmy's, drank gin day and night and then flew off back to New York again. Why she spent almost a thousand dollars to come home and drink the same brand of gin she could get there is beyond me."

I wondered if Aunt Sis ever went to the corner store for mix, ever looked at the Southside Hills from Jim's kitchen window. Jimmy says she still had her black and orange hair, down to her waist, but that she always wrapped it up before coming out of the bedroom where she slept with her ninety-year-old mother.

Wish I could have seen her, cigarette between her lips, the curling smoke making her eye pinch up as she folded out the cards in solitaire, and sloshed the plastic stirrer into gin and ice.

Lillian

Everyone wanted to get away. There was a whole slew of us lined up, signing our names on visa applications. Above all else — get out. Why turn over one more maggoty fish, iron one more shirt, scrub one more floor for two dollars a month? Give me a warm Jewish restaurant on Eighth Avenue where you get respect and tips.

Aunt Lil worked hard, married Pete Wasinski. I remember him in the grass, under the dogberry tree, coins falling from his pockets like bread crumbs, laughing as the wind stood his hair up straight. Mom said that when he died the shoes blew off his feet from his massive heart attack. Well, he did have such a big heart, making sure we kids found the silver in the grass.

Aunt Lil married again, a man from home. Came back to Newfoundland saying she could never stay in the States any more: "All the small town feel is gone from Manhattan."

Lillian, oldest daughter, never had children or a pet, but has a full-length sealskin coat. "The only thing your grandmother gave us," she told me, "was longevity and guts. That was all she gave us."

Ellen

In the snapshot she has her sweater pinned at the neck, but her arms aren't in the sleeves. This strikes me as unlike her so I look for more. It is some sort of courtyard where she stands, drooping veronicas are lined against a black fence. Her smile is a question of delight, like when someone says, "You are beautiful," and you say, "What?" because you want to hear it again.

The wind is blowing in the photo, her skirt tail is kicking up behind her. At her feet a small dog barks silently and she leans into a man who looks like Trotsky (he stayed at the Cochrane Hotel on his way to Mexico, and she worked next door).

I asked her about this once and she gave me that smile again and brushed her fingers across her lips as if the room was bugged. "Facts," she said. "Oh my, why do you always need the facts, you with all these photographs?"

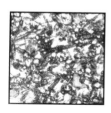

Sharon Puddester is a visual artist who lives in St. John's. After graduation from Memorial University, she went on to the Fine Arts programs at Capilano College, North Vancouver, B.C. and the University of Sydney in Australia. She has had several solo exhibitions, including *A Part of the Landscape: A Part of the Energy* at the Art Gallery of Newfoundland and Labrador in 1995, and *A Part of the Landscape* at the Christina Parker Fine Art Gallery in 1993. She is currently the Director of St. Michael's Printshop in St. John's.

Mary Dalton is an Associate Professor of English at Memorial University. She has published two volumes of poetry, *The Time of Icicles* (Breakwater, 1989) and *Allowing the Light* (Breakwater, 1993). She co-edited *Wild on the Crest: Sea Poems: Newfoundland and Labrador* (Jeroboam, 1995). Her essay on the symbolism of Gerald Squires' *Boatman* paintings appeared recently in *Newfoundland Studies*.

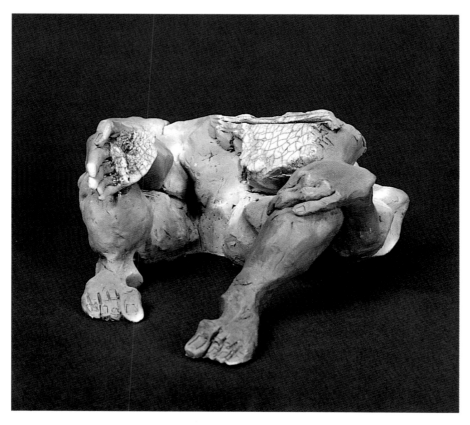

Sod, 1989
raku fired clay sculpture, 9½ x 11 x 5 in (24 x 28 x 13 cm), private collection
(photos: Memorial University Photographic Services)

Raku: Sod

for Sharon Puddester

Fire cannot bee hid in the straw, nor the nature of man
so concealed, but at last it will have his course.
—Thomas Lodge, *Rosalynde*

Wodge. Lump. Clod.
Riddle me.

Riddle me. My mothers:
Clay and fire and straw
And the shaper's hands.

Hands on/of sod. Seething of earth
Out of, into, up from
The clay mother, her turfy
Enticements. Let me out.

Let me out: knead, slap, tear—
Knobs, hollows, gouges—
You caving, I am forming myself,
You are finding me, I am bubbling up,
Yeasty ferment twisting in your blood.

Twisting in blood out of bog and inferno
I am dragging myself up dragging you are
You being that surges
Out into, along with
The breathing, you breathe, I am breathing—
Who is roiling here into birth?

Who roils along my clayey flanks
Swelling them to muscle bulging
Great hams and calves, the taut
And eloquent feet, clenched into, against
The pull downward, the mother I must
Wrestle out of, the mother I must
Know, my own spores, while writhing out of her?

Writhing out of her, my back a gleaming furrow,
Mica glints on field, my potato beginnings,
And the lifting, I am shaping myself
Out of my own being, the hand, yes, my hand
Poised to augment, augment. Moving into a
Face out of that cracked glaze, broken time.
The infinite, taut moment: creating, dissolving.

The taut moment: here Adam, Antaeus
And Caliban gather. A ghost in the future,
Rodin's thinker beckons. My mother laughs,
Calls me home, down. Her mud-crooning
Bathes me in the warm dark. Still I go on.
The pulse of fire burns in me now.
My hand will rise slowly to the hacked and broken mosaic,
There where my eyes will glimpse their own image,
There where my mouth will pour out its song.

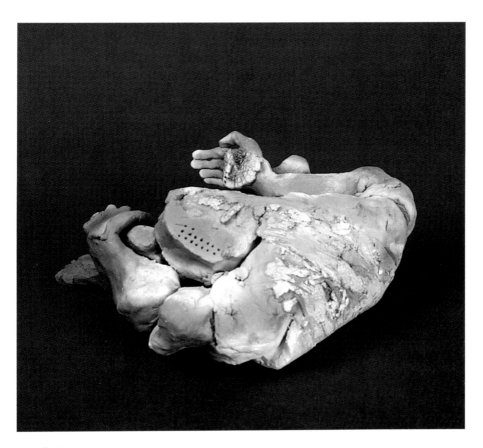

Sod

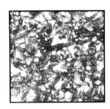 **Shawn Steffler** was born in Toronto in 1950. She received her Bachelor of Fine Arts at the University of Guelph, her Bachelor of Education in Art at the University of Toronto and her Master of Fine Arts at the University of Waterloo. Since 1975 Steffler has lived in Corner Brook, Newfoundland where she is a practising artist, art teacher and illustrator of children's books. Steffler has exhibited widely and her work is in the collections of the Canada Council Art Bank, Memorial University, Government of Newfoundland and Labrador and the University of Waterloo.

Joan Clark, who in 1991 received The Marian Engel Award for a body of work, is the author of two adult short story collections, two adult novels and seven children's books. Clark was the recipient of The Hawthornden Fellowship in 1994 and The Canada-Scotland Award in 1992. Her 1988 novel *The Victory of Geraldine Gull* was shortlisted for the Governor-General's Fiction Award and the W.H. Smith Award and won the Canadian Authors' Association Fiction Award. *Eiriksdottir, A Tale of Dreams & Luck*, a novel set in l'Anse Aux Meadows, Newfoundland, was first published in 1994 and is now a Penguin paperback. Clark's most recent book, *The Dream Carvers*, a young adult novel published by Viking/Puffin, received the 1995 Geoffrey Bilson Award for Historical Fiction for Young People. She is presently working on a stage play and a novel.

Shawn Steffler

Unspeakable Secrets, 1987
acrylic on paper, 16 x 20 in (40.6 x 51 cm), collection: Joan Clark
(photo: Ned Pratt)

Unspeakable Secrets: A Play in 7 Scenes
The stage is a giant's subliminal mind.
Five beetle-like Secrets scuttle onstage, speaking in a metallic whine.

SCENE 1

— Hey, Idie baby, do you know where we are?
— My guess is an island in the sub-continent.
— Sub-conscious, you mean.
— Wherever. Somewhere in the sun.
— That's the moon, Idie baby. *(Alter edges closer.)* Makes me horny.
   Feel like a little ummmmm . . . rub-a-dub-dub?

SCENE 2

— Time to rattle the cage, fellas.
— Fellas, he said, tee-hee.
— Use the video.
— You want to see before or after my sex change?
— Was there a slip-up, Froid? Is that half an udder you got hanging there?
— Those are penis twins, Idie.
— Jeez, no wonder you've been banished.

SCENE 3

— Is this a prison colony?
   I can't believe I was shipped down here for picking my nose.

SCENE 4

— Listen, girls . . .
— Boys . . .
— Listen, anyway. Let's pool our marbles and break outta here.
— But we're helpless! Look at us: we've been dis-armed!
— Ah, but we have Sin on our side.

— Not to mention Guilt.

— What we do is kick up such a ruckus that he . . .

— She . . .

— The sleeping giant will kick us out!

SCENE 5

— Altogether now, let's awaken that brain! One, Two, Three,
   as loud as you can:

— I had a sex change!

— I picked my nose!

— I was in love with my mother!

— I slept with my sister's Barbie!

— I was Darth Vader's mistress!

There is a prolonged primal wail and the five Secrets scurry for the cover of the woods.

SCENE 6

— *(whispering)* Is it safe to come out of the woods, Ung?

— As long as we stay down under, we're okay.

— As long as we're unspeakable, you mean.

— Look at it this way, Eg, our job is to stage a nocturnal play.

— You mean this was all pretend?

— On the contrary. We are more real than those thoughts he . . .

— She . . .

— has during waking hours. We are so deadly, so lethal, there are two of us
   who can never appear. They must stay out *(marbles roll upward)* of the
   garden.

— Is that a joke?

SCENE 7

— Does this have anything to do with an apple?

— It has to do with ummmm . . . come close . . . Idie baby, come close. You too,
   Eg.

— Rub-a dub-dub!